AMAZING ARCHITECTURE
AMAZING STADIUMS

by Anita Nahta Amin

Ideas for Parents and Teachers

Pogo Books let children practice reading informational text while introducing them to nonfiction features such as headings, labels, sidebars, maps, and diagrams, as well as a table of contents, glossary, and index.

Carefully leveled text with a strong photo match offers early fluent readers the support they need to succeed.

Before Reading

- "Walk" through the book and point out the various nonfiction features. Ask the student what purpose each feature serves.
- Look at the glossary together. Read and discuss the words.

Read the Book

- Have the child read the book independently.
- Invite him or her to list questions that arise from reading.

After Reading

- Discuss the child's questions. Talk about how he or she might find answers to those questions.
- Prompt the child to think more. Ask: Have you ever been in a stadium? What features did you see?

Pogo Books are published by Jump!
5357 Penn Avenue South
Minneapolis, MN 55419
www.jumplibrary.com

Library of Congress Cataloging-in-Publication Data

Names: Amin, Anita Nahta, author.
Title: Amazing stadiums / by Anita Nahta Amin.
Description: Minneapolis, MN: Jump!, [2023]
Series: Amazing architecture
Includes index. | Audience: Ages 7-10
Identifiers: LCCN 2022011552 (print)
LCCN 2022011553 (ebook)
ISBN 9781636907475 (hardcover)
ISBN 9781636907482 (paperback)
ISBN 9781636907499 (ebook)
Subjects: LCSH: Stadiums—Juvenile literature.
Classification: LCC GV415 .A45 2023 (print)
LCC GV415 (ebook) | DDC 796.06/8—dc23/eng/20220421
LC record available at https://lccn.loc.gov/2022011552
LC ebook record available at https://lccn.loc.gov/2022011553

Editor: Eliza Leahy
Designer: Molly Ballanger

Photo Credits: Hrecheniuk Oleksii/Shutterstock, cover; Martin D. Vonka/Shutterstock, 1; Tom Wang/Shutterstock, 3; fstop123/iStock, 4; Chris Owens/Shutterstock, 5; Cris Foto/Shutterstock, 6-7; Christian Bertrand/Shutterstock, 8; stellalevi/iStock, 9; Eric Broder Van Dyke/Shutterstock, 10-11; Hufton+Crow-VIEW/Alamy, 12-13; lev radin/Shutterstock, 14-15 (top); Leonard Zhukovsky/Shutterstock, 14-15 (bottom); superjoseph/iStock, 16; Chintung Lee/Shutterstock, 17; Jborzicchi/Dreamstime, 18-19; A.P.S. (UK)/Alamy, 20-21; Paparacy/Shutterstock, 23.

Printed in the United States of America at Corporate Graphics in North Mankato, Minnesota.

Title Page Image: Main Olympic Stadium, Greece

TABLE OF CONTENTS

Kaohsiung National Stadium, Taiwan

CHAPTER 1

BUILDING BIG

Stadiums can be used for many events, such as concerts. They are mostly used for sporting events. Fans watch teams play. They cheer from the **stands**.

fans

Stadiums are large. The Indianapolis Motor Speedway in Indiana can fit 350,000 fans. Fourteen football stadiums could fit inside!

Indianapolis Motor Speedway

crane

Architects design stadiums. They make **blueprints**. Then, they work with **engineers** to make sure stadiums will be strong. Construction workers build stadiums. They use cranes to lift and place heavy pieces.

DID YOU KNOW?

For safety, stadiums must be easy to get around. Sections are numbered. This helps people find their seats. There must be many doors. Why? This allows people to leave quickly if there is an emergency.

EXIT

CHAPTER 2

STADIUMS AT WORK

Architects plan for how many fans will be in a stadium. Seats get higher the farther away from the field they are. Why? This lets fans see over the people in front of them.

Stadiums are big to fit many people. This also means they are heavy. Just a roof can weigh more than 1 million pounds (450,000 kilograms)! The **structure** must hold the **load** of the roof, floors, and fans.

column ┄┄┄►

Columns, arches, and walls support the load. The load pushes down to the **foundation**. Many foundations have **piles**. These also support the load.

TAKE A LOOK!

How is load supported in a stadium? Take a look!

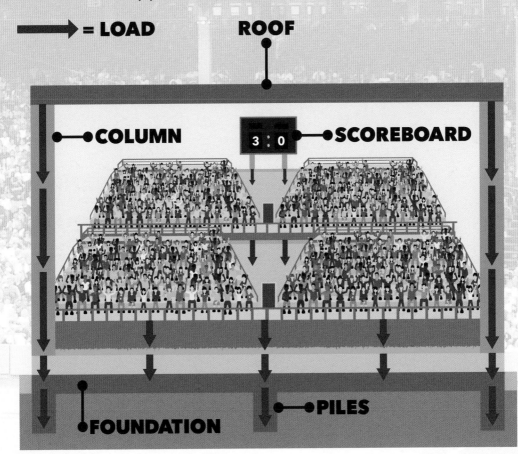

= LOAD

ROOF

COLUMN

SCOREBOARD

3 : 0

FOUNDATION

PILES

panel

Stadiums get loud. Announcers talk over speakers. Music plays. Fans cheer.

Stadiums are designed to **reflect** sound back to fans' ears. **Sound waves** bounce off the walls. Some stadiums have roof **panels** that reflect sound.

Sunlight can make it hard for players and fans to see. Many stadiums are built so the players do not face the sun.

Rain or snow can ruin a game. Some stadiums have roofs that open and close. Arthur Ashe Stadium in New York City has one.

DID YOU KNOW?

Many stadiums have grass fields. Some fields can slide out of the buildings. How? They are on large trays with wheels. The grass gets the sun it needs to grow.

Arthur Ashe
Stadium

FAMOUS STADIUMS

Beijing National Stadium in China can fit 91,000 people. It weighs more than 5,500 elephants! Steel columns crisscross. They support the roof.

Beijing National Stadium

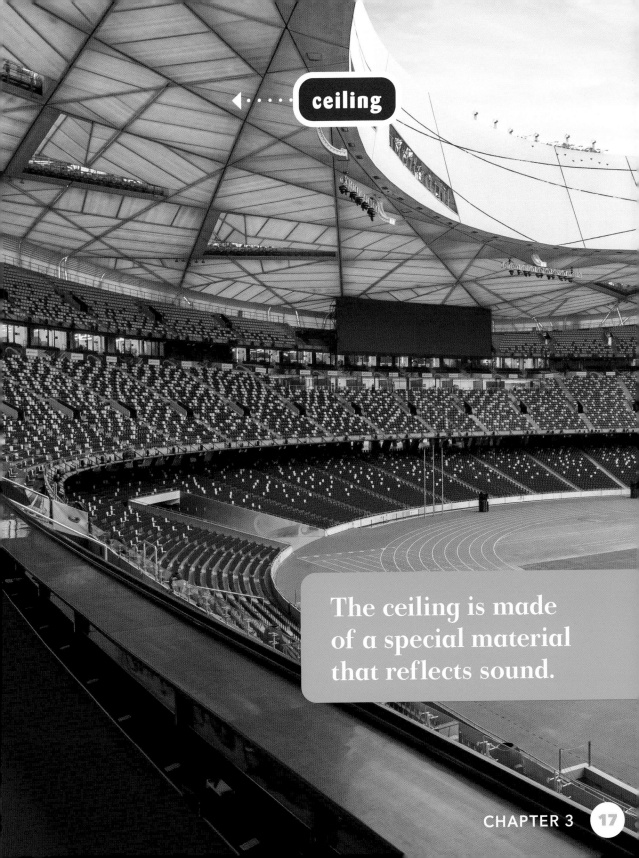

ceiling

The ceiling is made
of a special material
that reflects sound.

dome

CHAPTER 3

The National Sports Complex Olimpiyskiy is in Kiev, Ukraine. It has more than 70,000 seats.

The roof has 640 small **domes**. They let in light. **Cables** hold the domes in place. The cables are arranged like **spokes** in a wheel. They support the roof.

A steel arch is over Wembley Stadium in London, England. It holds the heavy roof up. The roof partly closes. It covers most of the stands. If it rains, the fans under it don't get wet!

Have you been to a stadium? What kind of amazing architecture did it have?

DID YOU KNOW?

Piles under Wembley Stadium go 115 feet (35 meters) deep in the ground. They support the heavy building.

arch · · · ·

ACTIVITIES & TOOLS

SUPPORT A ROOF

Stadium roofs are heavy. See how much support a roof needs with this fun activity!

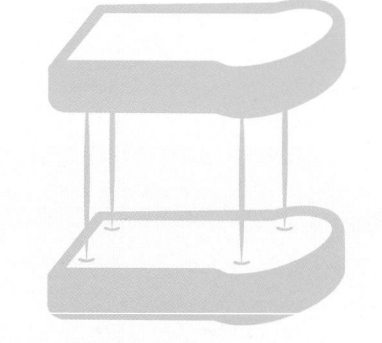

What You Need:
- four pretzel sticks or toothpicks
- slices of sandwich bread
- pencil or pen
- paper

1. **Stick one pretzel stick or toothpick into each of the four corners of one slice of bread. This will act as the foundation of your stadium.**

2. **Gently set another slice of bread on top of the pretzel sticks or toothpicks. Be careful not to break the supports. This is your roof. Does the structure collapse or stay up? Why do you think this is?**

3. **Make your roof heavier by adding more slices of bread on top. What happens to the structure as you add slices? Why do you think this is? Write down how many slices it takes for your stadium to collapse.**

4. **Make a stadium with other materials. Test how much weight it can hold. What do you notice?**

GLOSSARY

architects: People who design the look of structures.

blueprints: Models or detailed sketches of how structures will look.

cables: Thick ropes made of wires.

columns: Pillars that help support buildings.

domes: Parts of roofs that are shaped like half of a sphere.

engineers: People who are specially trained to design and build machines or large structures.

foundation: A solid base on which a structure is built.

load: The amount carried at one time.

panels: Flat pieces of wood or other materials made to form part of a surface such as a wall or roof.

piles: Heavy wood or steel beams that are driven into the ground to help support a structure.

reflect: To throw back heat, light, or sound from a surface.

sound waves: Waves or series of vibrations in the air, in a solid, or in a liquid that can be heard.

spokes: Thin rods that connect the rims of wheels to the hubs.

stands: Areas or rows of seats for fans at stadiums.

structure: Something that has been built.

Mercedes-Benz Stadium, Atlanta, Georgia

INDEX

TO LEARN MORE

Finding more information is as easy as 1, 2, 3.

1. **Go to www.factsurfer.com**
2. **Enter "amazingstadiums" into the search box.**
3. **Choose your book to see a list of websites.**

FACT SURFER